KROHN'S COMMENTARY OF THE BOOK
OF RUTH

BY

NICHOLAS M. KROHN

The King James Bible is the inspired, infallible, and living revelation of Almighty God for the English language. This commentary of the King James Bible is not. Through much reading and study of the Bible, this work is only my opinions and perspective. It is to be taken no further than that. Note that I may be wrong in some of my views in this commentary. I simply pray this will be a spiritual help to those who read it.

Dedicated to Ruth Hoffman.

A most dear and wonderful lady that shows the fruit of the Spirit on a daily basis and has been an overflowing source of compassion and kindness throughout the entire time I have known her.

All biblical quotes are taken from the King James Bible. No variations have been made, save for the capitalization of all pronouns that refer to the Lord so as to add reverence to His holy name. All underlines to Bible verses have been added to emphasize certain portions of the verses.

Many Hebrew words are referenced throughout this book. I acknowledge that I am not an expert in this language but am using Strong's Greek and Hebrew Dictionary to find the words that were originally used in the writing of the Scriptures. If there are any errors regarding the use of the Hebrew language, I sincerely apologize and would also encourage personal study of the Bible rather than fully trusting my words on these subjects.

TABLE OF CONTENTS

The book of Ruth begins during the time when the judges were the authorities in Israel. Though there are many speculations as to which judge was ruling during the story of Ruth (such as Gideon,[1] Ehud, or Deborah), it is not entirely certain since the judge is not referenced at all. All in all, it is of little consequence as to which judge was in authority because he or she had no significant impact on the lives of any of the characters within this account.

Everything was set in motion when a famine came to Israel. Quite a peculiar thing for the land flowing with milk and honey to have a famine, or the fact that Bethlehem itself means "house of bread," yet bread was in short supply. But the time of the judges was not a godly time. In fact, some of Israel's darkest accounts

_____

1. Gideon is believed by some to be the judge at this time since the Midianites "destroyed the increase of the earth" and "left no sustenance for Israel," (Judges 6:4) causing a man-made famine, which could have been the same famine mentioned in Ruth. Furthermore, it would have given Elimelech all the more reason to leave Israel since the Midianites were invading.

were in the time of the judges. There were periods where a judge would lead the people back to God, but the people would ultimately fall back into wickedness as soon as that judge passed off the scene. That being said, the famine was likely a form of judgment from the Lord, as He said would happen if His people would not hearken to Him:

"But if ye will not hearken unto Me, and will not do all these commandments;…And I will break the pride of your power; and I will make your heaven as iron, and your earth as brass: And your strength shall be spent in vain: for your land shall not yield her increase, neither shall the trees of the land yield their fruits."

(Leviticus 26:14, 19 – 20)

Because of this, a man of the tribe of Ephraim, Elimelech, took his family and set out to go live in the land of Moab. Though he was doing what he thought was best for his family, he was sadly in the wrong. Now, had the Lord commanded Elimelech to take his family to Moab, that would have been a different story entirely. However, we find no command from God. We don't even find any evidence of Elimelech praying to God for guidance or provision. Rather, Elimelech seemed to simply forsake the promised land and journeyed into heathen territory. Secular thinking says that this was the right and logical thing to do, but wisdom recognizes this as a very dangerous move. Abraham also sojourned to Egypt without the Lord's guidance and that led to the situation with Hagar and Ishmael. Secular thinking proclaimed that Abraham's journey to Egypt and his dealings with Hagar were reasonable, but wisdom shows that this was all for the worse. The massive amounts of warfare and unrest in the Middle-East today are between the descendants of Isaac and the descendants of Ishmael. And, for Elimelech, wisdom was shown to be correct in the end as well. Elimelech exchanged one dearth for three deaths. This is a warning that all husbands and fathers ought to heed. The very best thing you can do for your family is to lead them into the place of God's will. If you do anything besides that, you are actively harming your own family.

Now, some might ask what was so wrong with going into Moab. Well, Moab may have had food, but it also had pagan gods. Moab was a land known for its immorality and idolatry. In Numbers 25:1, Israel committed fornication with the women of Moab. The book of Revelation tells us that it was Balaam's counsel to the Moabite king, Balak, to use women to seduce Israel into sin:

"But I have a few things against thee, because thou hast there them that hold the doctrine of Balaam, who taught Balac to cast a stumblingblock before the children of Israel, to eat things sacrificed unto idols, and to commit fornication."

(Revelation 2:14)[2]

Moreover, in Judges 10:6, the gods of Moab are specifically mentioned (among other nations' gods) to become a part of Israel's worship.[3] Elimelech was taking his family into a land that

---

2. Also see Numbers 22 – 31 for the account of Balaam and Balak.

3. I am not saying that Elimelech and his family existed during Judges 10, though it is a possibility.

was saturated with heathen customs, worship, and ideology. He was sacrificing the spiritual needs of his family for the physical needs. Providing the physical needs of your family *is* good and essential. Those who refuse to take care of their family are rightly condemned in the Bible:

"But if any provide not for his own, and specially for those of his own house, he hath denied the faith, and is worse than an infidel."

(1 Timothy 5:8)

However, if you throw out the spiritual needs for the sake of the physical, you are endangering the eternal state of your family members. Better to be a malnourished beggar going into heaven than a well-fed mizer going into hell. And though one could argue that Elimelech was desperate,[4] we do not find any other

---

4. And if he truly was desperate, turning to God for help would have certainly proven better than turning to Moab. The Lord has promised to be our refuge, our strength, and a very present help in times of trouble (Psalm 46:1).

inhabitants of Bethlehem following suit. Naomi is recognized by many Bethlehemites when she returns home. That means that they were there when she originally left. They had stayed in Bethlehem and it would appear that they had sufficient provision during the ten years.[5] That is not to say that they didn't experience very hard and challenging times, but they were still alive. The same could not be said of Elimelech, Mahlon, and Chilion. This also demonstrates the timeless truth that people are in far more danger outside of God's will than in it, even if God's will seems harder. God's will has often been compared to walled pavilion that protects all who take shelter in it. But many desert that pavilion for the open, desirable-looking fields outside. And all who do make themselves susceptible to the darts of the enemy, no longer being protected by the strong walls. Satan is a masterful hunter. He knows how to track, lure, and slay his prey with deadly efficiency. When you leave the safe pavilion of God's will, you give Satan a clear shot to snipe you dead in your tracks. This is

---

5. The Bible doesn't elaborate on their lives, so they could have lost family members as well, but the implication seems to be that they had not lost like Naomi had.

why life changes ought to be made with great amounts of prayer and godly counsel. Changing jobs, changing churches, moving to another state, taking out a significant loan, or things of like gravity should not be done on a whim. We ought to make sure God is going with us before making any kind of journey. How dreadful it is to find out later that you were walking in the footsteps of the tempter rather than the Saviour. That unfortunately appears to be what happened to Elimelech's family. But that does not mean the story is over, because God took their misery and molded it into something marvelous.

It was Elimelech's intention to only stay a little while in the land of Moab. Likely just until the famine passed. But that is how it always starts. Just a small step. Just a little compromise. Just a short time. But Elimelech passed before the famine did. We are not told how he died. His sons, now of marrying age, would have had the responsibility of headship of the family fall to them. And instead of staying only a short time in Moab, they stayed for an entire decade. When they took Ruth and Orpah as their wives, the passage shows no evidence that the women were required to forsake the Moabite gods and worship the God of Israel. Rather, it appears that Mahlon and Chilion were assimilating into Moabite culture and forsaking the true and living God.[6] This was contrary to what God had commanded:

"When the LORD thy God shall bring thee into the land whither thou goest to possess it, and hath cast out many nations before thee, the Hittites, and the Girgashites, and the Amorites, and the Canaanites, and the Perizzites, and the Hivites, and the Jebusites, seven nations greater and mightier than thou; And when the LORD thy God shall deliver them before thee; thou shalt smite them, *and* utterly destroy them; thou shalt make no covenant with them, nor shew mercy unto them: Neither shalt thou make marriages with them; thy daughter thou shalt not give unto his son, nor his daughter

---

6. It is a possibility that Mahlon and Chilion kept their Jewish heritage and identity, but we only see Ruth renounce her gods and believe in Jehovah God when she adamantly decided to stay with Naomi (Ruth 1:16). Thus, it is more likely that Naomi was the one who stayed faithful to the Lord while her sons may have shifted to whatever degree in Moabite culture.

shalt thou take unto thy son. For they will turn away thy son from following Me, that they may serve other gods: so will the anger of the LORD be kindled against you, and destroy thee suddenly."

(Deuteronomy 7:1 – 4)[7]

The Lord gave them ten years to get things right. As stated before, Mahlon and Chilion were now the heads of the home. The responsibility fell on them. God always looks to the man of the house as the authority. And when Mahlon and Chilion, at best, neglected to correct their father's mistake or, at worst, abandoned the Lord for the gods of Moab, they passed away as well. Though, upon looking into what their names mean, it may not have been all that surprising at the time. For Mahlon means "weak" or "sick," and Chilion means "destruction" or "consumption." Not exactly the most popular baby name meanings. It is inferred that

---

7. Though Moab is not specifically mentioned in the list of the countries that the Israelites were not to marry, the principle still follows that if someone was going to marry, their God had to be the Lord and not a heathen, false god. Again, we find no evidence that Ruth and Orpah were forced to give up their gods.

these two boys were not the most hardy or healthy, but were rather

sickly in their upbringing. On that note, I feel that I must address

that there are many who dogmatically state that God brought

divine judgment upon these two boys when they didn't return to

the place of God's will. Though that could very likely be the case,

I feel that it should be emphasized that the Bible does not clearly

state that this was punishment of the Lord as it does with

individuals like Er (Genesis 38:7) or Herod (Acts 12:21 – 23).

The Lord has no obligation to protect us from our own poor

choices. After all, Moab did not adhere to the dietary and sexual

laws of Israel, which caused much more sickness, unhealthy

lifestyles, and shorter lifespans. If Elimelech, Mahlon, and

Chilion started living according to how Moabites did, their lives

could have been shortened dramatically (especially if Mahlon and

Chilion were already of a weaker constitution). I do believe that

the Lord's blessing was removed from Mahlon and Chilion's lives because of their decision to stay in Moab,[8] but their deaths may have simply been consequences of their own choices.

Every choice you make can have unforeseen consequences. That is why it is so crucial to be in constant communication and fellowship with the Lord. Elimelech had no idea that the decision to leave Bethlehem would cost him his life, as well as the life of his two boys. And you and I today have no idea just what may be around the bend of any decision that we make. So speak to God often, submit your plans to Him, and be willing to change your plans to His. If you refuse to change your decision when He asks you to change, the results could be much more dire than you perceive.

_____

8. There is further evidence of this by the fact that neither Mahlon nor Chilion had any children during their entire marriage to Ruth and Orpah. Now, we don't know when in the ten years the boys married the two Moabite women, but if it was nearer to the beginning of the ten years, I could very well see that as God withholding the blessing of children due to their disobedience.

It is important to not simply read over verse 5. Naomi lost her husband and two sons. This is a devastating situation to be in and it is not to be read without grave and humble consideration. Anyone going through such loss would be tempted to grow as bitter as Naomi did. Perhaps even worse. Now, I am not saying that I condone such bitterness at all. However, I do understand it. Many times, modern believers can have the mindset of "Well, I would have done better if I had been in that situation" when it comes to Biblical accounts. Let us not be so lofty to say that we would not react similarly. I know that if I were to suddenly lose my wife and children, my heart would be shattered. I would be tempted to lash out at God, though I would hope I would respond more like Job. However, I do not believe I can really say what I would do without actually experiencing it, though I pray I never do.

Moving on, note that Naomi did not share in the fate of Elimelech, Mahlon, or Chilion. Why was this? Because when the responsibility finally fell to her (there was no longer an adult man in the household, so she held the most authority, being the mother-in-law),[9] Naomi returned to the place of God's will and therefore did not suffer death like her husband or sons. Though the Bible tells us that she began her return to Bethlehem only after hearing that there was bread again, the important aspect is that she did return. She could have very easily remained where she was in Moab. Instead, she trekked back to the land of her nativity and the land of her God.

---

9. Though this is not popular in today's culture and considered misogynistic, the Lord has set it up that the man of the household is the authority. This does not mean that the man of the household ought to be mean, cruel, or unfair in his authority. He is held accountable of God to be a just and caring authority that will guide his family in the right way. This also does not mean that the woman is without a voice. In my own relationship with my wife, I never like to make decisions without first speaking with her. She sees situations in a light I do not and is often times much smarter than I am. But at the end of the day, it is up to me to make the decision and to make it with God's will at the center of it. And it is up to my wife to honor and accept that decision. Note to the men: use great caution when making crucial decisions. For you could lead your family to Moab (speaking figuratively) and devastate your family just like Elimelech did.

Originally, both Orpah and Ruth wished to go with Naomi. This demonstrates how tender the relationship was between these two women and their mother-in-law. They were willing to forsake their blood relatives and the land of their birth rather than abandon the mother of their husbands. This speaks volumes. Now, many daughter-in-laws have wonderful relationships with their mother-in-laws, and vice versa. However, how many daughters-in-law today, after losing their husband, would decide to move in with their mother-in-law rather than go back to their blood family? I would wager not many. But Ruth and Orpah were willing to do so. They must have truly loved their mother-in-law very fervently. And not love only, but also a great deal of respect. Notice how neither Ruth nor Orpah pleaded with Naomi for her to remain in Moab. They respected her wishes to return to Israel and were willing to follow her. Naomi had shown herself such a delightful part of their life that they wished to not lose her as well. Wherever Naomi was going to be, they were going to be there with her. We, as Christians, ought to strive to be such compassionate and kind people that the lost might wish to cling to us as well.[10]

Naomi, however, discouraged Ruth and Orpah's company. For the first discouragement, Ruth and Orpah both stayed steadfast and were determined to continue with Naomi. But Naomi discouraged further. Thinking much like her husband had, she focused on the physical and the logical at the expense of the spiritual:

1. Naomi had no husband to bear more sons.

2. The likeliness of Naomi marrying again and bearing children was acutely small. She was believed to be around fifty years

---

10. Just to clarify, this does not mean that just because we are kind and compassionate that the lost will not be antagonistic to us. We need to remember that Jesus said "If ye were of the world, the world would love his own: but because ye are not of the world, but I have chosen you out of the world, therefore the world hateth you." (John 15:19) This also does not mean that getting the lost to like us should be our supreme goal. If we make being liked our goal, we will be tempted to compromise God's truth in order to attain it.

old, which was not too old for marrying and not impossible for bearing children, but very unlikely.

3. Even if Naomi was to marry that night and get pregnant that very night, she would not only have to have twins, but they would have to be twin boys.

4. Even if Naomi was able to bear twin boys, Ruth and Orpah would have to wait nearly two decades until they could marry them.

5. "The Lord is gone out against me" – Naomi believed that the Lord was opposing her and that, if Ruth and Orpah came with her, the Lord would oppose them as well.

Naomi believed they would be better off finding Moabite husbands to provide for them now rather than stick with an Israelite widow. She did not seem to consider the fact that the Lord is Jehovah-Jireh. That God provides for those who follow

Him. He provides better than any husband ever could. And Ruth would live to see that. Unfortunately, Orpah did not.[11] Orpah took in Naomi's words and realized that, logically speaking, Naomi was right. What Israelite would take Orpah as a wife? The Israelites and Moabites were long-standing enemies. In Israel, the probability for Orpah to remain a widow was great. Not only that, but the odds were in favor of her being ostracized and prejudiced against for her Moabite heritage. Furthermore, Naomi had no way of providing for herself, let alone two daughters-in-law with her. The risk that came with staying with Naomi was too high. And, thus, she kissed her mother-in-law goodbye.

We never hear of Orpah again in Scripture. I would like to believe that she held to the light of Naomi's God even while going back to Moab. However, at the end of the day, we have no idea. The Bible doesn't say. The important thing for us to take from this is that Naomi was both the person that introduced Orpah to the true God and the person that pushed her away from the true God.

---

11. That we know of.

We, as Christians, need to be mindful that we can be the very instruments that keep people from getting saved when we use logic at the expense of being spiritually-minded. Naomi was trying to do what she thought was best for Orpah and Ruth, but she actually paved the path that led to paganism and utter hopelessness for Orpah. Let us learn from this passage and not continue paving that same path for others in our day and time. When tempted to be overwhelmed by our surrounding circumstances, we must turn our eyes to the Lord. He is able to overcome any obstacle, any difficulty, and any sorrow. And, in those times of difficulty, our response may be the very thing that either wins the lost to the Lord or forever confirms their skepticism towards Him. If we respond in faith, even when it doesn't make sense with our terrible situation, that shows that our relationship with Jesus is real to those who don't believe. But, if we crack and crumble under the pressure and trade in the spiritual for the logical, that shows the lost that there is nothing special about our faith and that we will drop it at the first sign of trouble. And if that is how a Christian behaves, why would the lost be inclined to follow Jesus? Christianity would appear to be no different from any other religion. We need to take time to really contemplate this passage so as to not repeat it.

Ruth had a completely different response to Naomi's discouragements than Orpah did. When Orpah gave in to the secular logic of Naomi's words and decided to return to Moab, Ruth instead did the opposite and clave unto Naomi. This word "clave" comes from the Hebrew word "דָּבַק" (pronounced "daw-bakʺ"), which means "to cling or adhere to, to catch by pursuit, abide." It is the same word that is used in Genesis 2:24 – "Therefore shall a man leave his father and his mother, and shall **_cleave_** unto his wife: and they shall be one flesh." Ruth's commitment was so strong to Naomi, the same word that describes God's idea of marital commitment was used for her dedication to her mother-in-law.[12] Just take a look at Ruth's words:

"Intreat me not to leave thee, or to return from following after thee: for whither thou goest, I will go; and where thou lodgest, I will lodge: thy people shall be my people, and thy God my God: Where thou diest, will I die, and there will I be buried: the LORD do so to me, and more also, if ought but death part thee and me."

(Ruth 1:16 – 17)

---

12. This, of course, does not mean there was anything romantic between the two individuals. Normally, I wouldn't have to state this (especially since Ruth and Naomi were related by marriage), but with the homosexual movement nowadays, I felt it was necessary. It is honestly quite sad that many tender moments between two people of the same gender are instantly chalked up to being something of a homosexual nature. Once upon a time, men and women were able to show their own gender tenderness and platonic love without worry of being considered homosexual. It is still right for people to have this kind of close bond with one another without it being romantic. Ruth and Naomi shared this kind of affection as well as others in the Bible. This included David and Jonathan, Jesus with the twelve, Paul and Barnabas, and others. The Lord designed us to have close, intimate friendships with those of our own gender as well, so let us not allow culture to keep us from having them.

This statement from Ruth is renowned by many as one of the greatest declarations in the Old Testament. And what faith! To leave behind everything she had known and commit to living as an Israelite. I really wish we had just a little more insight as to why Ruth responded this way even after Naomi tried to dissuade her. Was it because she had seen Naomi's faith previously during their lives together? Was it because Naomi demonstrated how God was real when all of the gods of Moab proved to be false and silent? We don't know, nor is it truly the point. The point is that Ruth made a decision to stick by Naomi's side and worship Naomi's God. And she steeled her resolve to stay true to that decision.

Naomi could see that there was no further point in arguing to try and convince Ruth to stay in Moab. Naomi had seen that Ruth was "steadfastly minded," which could actually be translated "hard-headed." There are times in our lives where it is best for us to be hard-headed concerning a few things. Though it sounds a little backwards, stubbornness can be a great tool used of the

Lord. When others try to persuade us to engage in something sinful or dangerous, sanctified stubbornness is the right response. When authority tells us to stop doing that which God has called us to do (witnessing, praying, reading our Bible, etc.), sanctified stubbornness is again the right path. Now, I am not saying it is right to be mean or nasty concerning the matter, but show those individuals that you are "steadfastly minded" in the same way Ruth showed Naomi. Ruth was kind about it, but she was essentially saying "I know what you want me to do, but, with all due respect, I'm not going to."

Ruth and Naomi journeyed together from Moab to Bethlehem. The journey could have been anywhere from ninety to over one hundred fifty miles,[13] depending where they started from in Moab. They would have had to go north back into Israel through the tribe of Reuben, then travel west through the tribe of Benjamin, and finally travel south into the tribe of Judah to Bethlehem. The reason they would have to travel in such a way instead of a straight line is because the Dead Sea was between them and Bethlehem. Naturally, they had to go around it, but probably would not have gone the southern route since they would have had to venture into Edom and add unnecessary danger to their journey.

If there were any dangers or eventful happenings on their trek from Moab to Bethlehem, it is not recorded in Scripture.

---

13. Measurements taken from a modern GPS. They may be slightly off since I was going by modern cities in Jordan. Parts of Jordan are modern-day Moab.

This, I find, is rather remarkable. Remember, this was during the time of the book of Judges, which was one of the most ungodly times in the Old Testament. However, depending on what point of Judges they were in makes a great deal of difference. For there were times of repentance and peace when a godly judge was on the scene. If Ruth and Naomi's time was during one of those instances, this makes much more sense why they would have had a journey without any trouble. But we also know that there were some very dark times during Judges where it was even dangerous for *men* to travel through Israel, let alone two ladies by themselves. All in all, I believe that God was directing their way and protecting their path as they walked from Moab to Bethlehem. After all, what could have been a seven to ten day arduous journey was summarized in one sentence with "So they two went until they came to Bethlehem."

Once Ruth and Naomi arrived in Bethlehem, it caused quite a stir. It can sometimes be overlooked that Bethlehem was a very small town. It likely had a population of maybe 2,000 or 3,000 people. Now, it has grown to a population of 28,591[14] in our modern times, but it was just a small village back in the days of the Old Testament. Even when Jesus was born, it was no large city. And so, in small towns, everyone generally knows everyone else. That is why the Bethlehemites started murmuring about Naomi when she walked back into town after being gone for a decade.

It is from verse 19 that we can discern that Naomi's appearance had drastically changed since she was last in Bethlehem. For people who knew her previously to be asking each other "Is *this* Naomi?" says quite a bit. I imagine that it dealt with one of two things:

1. Naomi dramatically aged physically due to her loss. Emotional and/or mental trauma can affect one's physical appearance in a very ill fashion. Examples of this can be found in photos of war veterans before and after engaging in

---

14. Population as of 2017.

warfare, as well as presidents of the United States of America before and after their four year term.

2. Naomi was so depressed and so readily wore her sorrow on her face that her present countenance reflected very little of the Naomi ten years prior. This would probably be more the case if Naomi had been known as a very cheerful, merry, and jovial woman in her past.

It could very well have been both, which would compound how different she looked. And when Naomi noticed the stares and mutters from the townspeople, she displayed her bitterness and her hurt through her words:

"Call me not Naomi, call me Mara: for the Almighty hath dealt very bitterly with me. I went out full, and the LORD hath brought me home again empty: why *then* call ye me Naomi, seeing the LORD hath testified against me, and the Almighty hath afflicted me?"

(Ruth 1:20 – 21)

There are glaring issues with Naomi's little declaration. However, we still need to remember that she was hurting deeply. She lost her husband and two sons. And those who are hurting often aren't thinking clearly and are looking for someone to blame. That being said, it was not right of her to accuse God of robbing her of her family. This statement paints God as a villainous character. It depicts Him of being an unjust slayer of Elimelech, Mahlon, and Chilion without any substantial reason. God may not have even been behind it at all, for I must again iterate that the Bible does not specify that the three deaths were due to divine judgment. It could have simply been results from living in the much less healthy culture of Moab, which would have merely been the consequences of the choice to move there. If that was the case, there is no foundation at all to blame God. Now, if their deaths were the result of heavenly retribution, God is still blameless because He was only being just when Elimelech, Mahlon, and Chilion refused to listen to His Word.

Naomi no longer wished to be called "pleasant," which is what "Naomi" means. She was bitter and so she wished to be called "bitter." This is what "Mara" means. Her bitterness had already done some damage to those around her. She had turned Orpah away due to being bitter against the Lord. She had attempted to do the same with Ruth, though Ruth persevered. Lastly, she spoke ill of the Lord to her fellow Bethlehemites, though we do not see their response to her words. Even though she was caught up in her sorrow and her bitterness, God did not abandon her. The final verse of chapter one shows a ray of hope:

"So Naomi returned, and Ruth the Moabitess, her daughter in law, with her, which returned out of the country of Moab: and they came to Bethlehem in the beginning of barley harvest."

(Ruth 1:22)

First, it is good to note that it is emphasized that Naomi returned out of Moab. God allows us the freedom to venture where we may. We can stay by His side or stray to places like Moab.[15] We are free to make those kind of choices, but we are not free to choose our consequences. However, at the end of the day, we can choose to come back from Moab. Like the prodigal son, we can return to the Father, ask for His forgiveness, and He will receive us with open arms and celebrate our return. But there is another point to this verse that shows good things on the horizon: "and they came to Bethlehem in the beginning of barley harvest." This would have been Israel's first harvest after the winter, usually taking place around late March or April. It marked the end

_____

15. I, of course, mean this figuratively. Moab is being used as a reference to something outside of God's will for you. Though, it is vitally important in our lives to be in the physical place God wishes us to be.

of the famine that Israel had been in. Furthermore, it gave Naomi and Ruth an opportunity to sustain themselves. Neither Naomi nor Ruth could necessarily go out and get themselves a job, per se. That was reserved for the men in that time while the women took care of the household by way of cleaning, cooking, and child rearing.[16] This is why widows were so often destitute. But God had made provision for those who could not provide for themselves in the Law:

"And when ye reap the harvest of your land, thou shalt not wholly reap the corners of thy field, neither shalt thou gather the gleanings of thy harvest. And thou shalt not glean thy vineyard, neither shalt thou gather *every* grape of thy vineyard; thou shalt leave them for the poor and stranger: I *am* the LORD your God."

(Leviticus 19:9 – 10)

---

16. Note that I am merely stating the fact of how it was in that time, and not saying that women should be reserved only for cooking, cleaning, and taking care of kids. There is nothing wrong with any of those, should a woman be a stay-at-home mom, but it is understandable in our times and economy that both the husband and wife must work a job.

"And when ye reap the harvest of your land, thou shalt not make clean riddance of the corners of thy field when thou reapest, neither shalt thou gather any gleaning of thy harvest: thou shalt leave them unto the poor, and to the stranger: I *am* the LORD your God."

(Leviticus 23:22)

"When thou cuttest down thine harvest in thy field, and hast forgot a sheaf in the field, thou shalt not go again to fetch it: it shall be for the stranger, for the fatherless, and for the widow: that the LORD thy God may bless thee in all the work of thine hands. When thou beatest thine olive tree, thou shalt not go over the boughs again: it shall be for the stranger, for the fatherless, and for the widow. When thou gatherest the grapes of thy vineyard, thou shalt not glean *it* afterward: it shall be for the stranger, for the fatherless, and for the widow."

(Deuteronomy 24:19 – 21)[17]

---

17. Fun fact: Ruth qualifies as poor, a widow, a stranger, and fatherless. She's considered fatherless because she left her father behind in the land of Moab. At the time, she had no man as an authority or protector over her.

Now, it must be reminded that this was the time of the judges, where every man did that which is right in his own eyes rather than what was right in God's eyes. So not everyone was following the Law in the way that they should, but we'll get to more of that later. When it comes to the time of the arrival of Naomi and Ruth into Bethlehem, there could not have been a better time, it seems. The barley harvest was happening right as they walked into town. They wouldn't have to wait months for it and try and beg and scrounge until then. It also wasn't the only harvest to come, for the wheat harvest was to be immediately after the barley harvest. It's almost as if someone orchestrated Naomi and Ruth's lives so that they got to the right place at exactly the right time (wink, wink). And the account is about to get even better with the introduction of another individual in the next chapter.

The third main character of our biblical account enters the scene: Boaz. The first thing we are told about him is that he was a kinsman of Naomi's husband, Elimelech. Some may wonder why that fact was pertinent, but those within the Hebrew culture would have understood immediately that the author was building up for the kinsman redeemer. Now, what is the kinsman redeemer? This is spoken about in the Law:

"If brethren dwell together, and one of them die, and have no child, the wife of the dead shall not marry without unto a stranger: her husband's brother shall go in unto her, and take her to him to wife, and perform the duty of an husband's brother unto her. And it shall be, *that* the firstborn which she beareth shall succeed in the name of his brother *which is* dead, that his name be not put out of Israel."

(Deuteronomy 25:5 – 6)

In short, if a man died, his brother was to take his wife as his own and have relations with her until she was able to have a firstborn child. This may sound rather odd to us, perhaps even gross to us, but it was common and understood within the Hebrew culture. It was to ensure that the legacy of the dead husband continued and to guarantee that the widow would be taken care of. And so the second chapter of Ruth already starts implementing the idea of an upcoming marriage with the introduction of Boaz. He was not only a nearby kinsman, though, but was also a "mighty man of wealth." He had a significant amount of riches. He had more than enough means to take care of two widow women. God so often gives out blessings to us so that we may be a blessing to others. It is important to remember that when we find ourselves with an abundance of goods, it may be the Lord preparing us to be a help to someone who needs it.

Another thing to note about Boaz is that he was a single man, yet he was greatly used of God to make a difference in the lives of Naomi and Ruth. I say this to point out that a person does not have to be married to be used of God. There is an unfortunate mindset within many churches that single people are lesser than married individuals. Now, no one would say that outright (hopefully), but non-married folks have often felt that way. After all, some of the most favored Bible heroes were married during their time in the Bible spotlight:

- Abraham and Sarah

- Moses

- Deborah

- Hannah

- David

- Solomon

- Esther

- Job

- Mary

- Peter[18]

---

18. Contrary to Catholic belief, Peter was indeed married. Mark 1:30 – 31 says "But Simon's wife's mother lay sick of a fever, and anon they tell him of her. And he came and took her by the hand, and lifted her up; and immediately the fever left her, and she ministered unto them."

Combining this with the fact that there are so many other messages on marriage, married life, and the sexual relationship, single people can get the thought in their minds that they are not actually important until they get someone to wed them. But God values every person as they are and God can use single people sometimes even more so than married individuals. First, look at all the single people that God used in the Bible:[19]

- **Joseph** – God used him in Potiphar's house, used him to interpret the baker and butler's dreams, used him to interpret Pharaoh's dream, and used him to save Egypt and the surrounding nations in a time of great famine.
- **Rahab** – She demonstrated great faith and turned to Jehovah, which saved her and her entire family from the destruction of Jericho. She did all this as a single woman, for she married Salmon after the fall of Jericho.

---

19. Note that some of these individuals mentioned would be married in their life, but I am focusing on sections of their life when they were not and still used of God.

- **David** – He slew Goliath, his most well-known triumph, when he was a single teenager.

- **Daniel** – He never married, but was given numerous prophecies by God, including some for the end times. Also influenced Nebuchadnezzar, a wicked and barbarous king, to reverence the one true God.

- **Paul** – Probably the greatest human missionary of all time and writer of a vast amount of the New Testament.

And don't forget: Jesus was single, too. Maybe that's cheating, but it is a fact that Jesus never married and accomplished the greatest work of all time: salvation of all mankind through His shed blood on the cross of Calvary and His resurrection from the dead.

Ruth immediately got to work. Very admirable of the Moabitess to be eager to provide for herself and Naomi. She was likely informed by Naomi of how the poor could get themselves food by way of gleaning in the fields. Slight side note, but I like the fact that God instituted a type of work for the poor. Work is good for everyone, rich or poor, though we often think of it as a necessary evil.[20] However, God's idea for providing for the poor is to have them work for it. They are not to sit and do nothing all day while other people provided for them.[21] No, they worked in the field by gleaning that which was left behind. This was very simple work, but it was also very hard work. Contrary to that, the United States of America sadly has this very common image

---

20. We probably think of it as a necessary evil due to the curse that was placed upon work in Genesis 3:17 – 19. Work is still good and is still very much a satisfying aspect of humanity, but since Adam's sin, work has become *hard*. That, I think, may be why we dread it so much.

21. This shows that communism or socialism is not God's idea of government. Also, note that I am talking about the poor. I am not talking about those who cannot provide for themselves whether by disability, age, etc.

throughout the country: a person standing on a street corner with a cardboard sign that reads something like "Lost job. Have family to feed. Anything helps. God bless." Now, I worked in a Walmart parking lot for five years as a cart-pusher, and I can tell you that 99% of those people are not even remotely legitimate or genuine. I've seen countless "homeless" people begging on the side of the road get into a brand new suburban at the end of the day and drive off. I've heard someone with a sob story about how she ran out of gas and was trying to get back home (which was supposedly over an hour away), but I still saw her four months later telling that same story to someone else. Some of the time, those people even have to pay to stand on the particular street corner they're on. These are not people who are without means to work. Their reasoning may vary (don't want to get a job because it would force them to stop taking the drugs they are on, want to be able to get income without having to pay taxes on it, they find panhandling easy compared to a normal job, etc.) but it mostly comes down to the fact that they don't want to work honestly. How shameful. Additionally, it's hurting our country. At least the beggars in the time of Ruth went out and did honest work to provide for themselves rather than scheme and try to tug people's heartstrings to give them dishonest gain.[22]

Back to the text, Ruth went out to glean alone. I wonder why Naomi did not go with her. Naomi may have been older, but she is not believed to have been so old that she could not work. And it would have been better to have two glean in the fields than just one. This leads to a good deal of speculation of why Naomi refrained from gleaning:

1.   Naomi was prone to sickness like her sons were and was therefore too weak or sickly to work in the fields.

_____

22. Another note about this: don't encourage panhandlers by giving them money. If they want money, let them work a real job. In case you're worried they're the real deal, take solace that there are places where legitimate homeless and destitute people can go to get help, such as Open Door Mission, that will help them get back on their feet and get a job. If you don't believe me, just try giving one a meal instead of money. Many times, I've seen them reject a meal and again ask for money instead. This is because they don't actually have a problem with feeding themselves. Additionally, you don't know what they'll use that money for. They could use it for drugs or alcohol. All in all, giving cold hard cash to a panhandler isn't the best idea.

2. Naomi had other business to conduct while Ruth was out. This could have dealt with where they were currently living or perhaps she was even attempting to search out near kinsmen to aid with the affairs concerning Elimelech's land.

3. Naomi had allowed her depression to overwhelm her and simply made no effort to provide for herself or for Ruth, but reserved herself for a slow death of malnourishment.

We are not told, but whatever the reason, it was good that Ruth was there to aid Naomi. So, Ruth ventured out alone.

What Ruth was doing was potentially very dangerous. I believe she knew that, too. I cannot stress enough that this was in the time where every man did that which was right in his own eyes. A young woman walking the fields by herself was risky. Furthermore, she was no Israelite. She was a foreigner and it was apparently easy to tell.[23] Considering the fact that she was both a Moabitess and alone, any man could have attempted to do anything from hurting her to abusing her. Thank the Lord, none of that took place, though I wonder if she was run off from a few fields due to being a foreigner.

Regardless, "her hap was to light on a part of the field belonging unto Boaz." What does this mean when it says "hap"? The Hebrew word for this, "מִקְרֶה," (pronounced "mik-reh'") means "accident, fortune, or chance." The author is saying that Ruth *just so happened* to walk onto Boaz's field. Boaz, the man who not only was a near kinsman but a great man of integrity. Of course, the author is being ironic here, knowing full well that none of this was purely by chance. All these elements coming together in one moment is nothing less than a miracle. We know that God

---

23. Throughout the book, Ruth is never once found explaining her heritage. This could have been because she had some giveaway in her appearance, speech/dialect, or mannerisms. However, it also could be traced back to the fact that most everyone in Bethlehem directly or indirectly knew Naomi and simply connected the dots like so – "Naomi went to Moab and returned with a young woman. Naomi has no biological daughter, so the woman is obviously a Moabitess. Presumably a daughter-in-law that was married to one of Naomi's sons." It also could have been a mixture of the two.

was orchestrating her movements, leading her to just the right person at just the right time. As Ruth was working hard gleaning, Boaz arrived and began greeting his workers. Notice the exchange:

"And, behold, Boaz came from Bethlehem, and said unto the reapers, The LORD *be* with you. And they answered him, The LORD bless thee."

(Ruth 2:4)

This hints at Boaz's integrity and his dedication to the Lord. I understand that this could have been traditional only and said without any real conviction behind it. However, considering Boaz's attitude throughout the book, I believe he meant it when he said it. This also shows his diligence, because he did not have to come himself to see how the work proceeded. Verse 6 tells us that he had a servant that was set over the reapers. Yet, we see that Boaz himself came to supervise. In later passages, we even see him watching over the harvest in the middle of the night when he could have been taking his leisure elsewhere (Ruth 3:7). And, as he greeted his workers, Boaz noticed Ruth. With Bethlehem being a very small town, Boaz was probably relatively familiar with everyone. But this was a young woman he had never seen before. We start to notice the age difference between Ruth and Boaz by how he first queried of her:

"Then said Boaz unto his servant that was set over the reapers, Whose damsel _is_ this?"
(Ruth 2:5)

The Hebrew word for "damsel" is "נַעֲרָה," (pronounced "nah-ar-aw'") which refers to her as "a girl between infancy and adolescence." Now, Ruth wasn't a child. She was young, yes, but mature enough to have been of marrying age ten years prior. This means that she could have been anywhere from her mid-twenties to early thirties. So why did Boaz use this terminology for her? It would appear that Boaz simply saw her as a child when compared to his own age. Even in contemporary times, how often has a middle-aged person referred to a twenty-year-old as a child, baby, or kid? This is likely what happened when Boaz first saw Ruth.

Some people believe that Boaz was immediately taken with Ruth upon first seeing her. Due to the terminology he uses for Ruth, I am of the opinion that this wasn't the case. However, that is not to say that those who believe otherwise are necessarily wrong. The Bible doesn't give enough evidence to prove one way or the other. Furthermore, even if Boaz did have some immediate attraction to Ruth, the way he speaks of her hints that he was not going to act on it. He spoke of her like she was a child rather than a young woman.

All the same, Boaz was curious as to who this stranger was. Boaz was quickly updated by his servant as to who Ruth was and that she had been gleaning in the field all day. This is the point where I believe Boaz became quite impressed. He knew of Naomi and likely knew of her terrible situation. The fact that Ruth forsook her homeland and people for an elder widow woman, who could do nothing for her, spoke volumes. Furthermore, she showed herself to be a hard worker. There is a popular opinion among some that the women of the Bible were delicate and fragile. Odds are that some were, but certainly not Ruth. This is a woman that worked hard and worked long, much like the virtuous woman noted in Proverbs 31. She did not make frequent trips to the house to take her rest, but only "tarried a little" so as to get a fleeting moment of relief from the heat and the labor. We will see also in the coming passages that she had some strength about her, for not only did she work from morning until evening (this likely would have been ten to twelve hours of work), but she was able to carry an ephah of barley home with her. An ephah would have been about thirty to fifty pounds. She carried thirty to fifty pounds of barley all the way home with her. I'm not certain how far the walk was back to Naomi, but I doubt it was right around the corner.

Throughout much of this book, we are shown what it means to have a good work ethic. One would expect such morals to be expounded upon in Proverbs rather than Ruth, yet we see it here anyway. Humorously enough, Proverbs would not have existed had not Ruth worked hard.[24] Ruth would not have met Boaz had she not been willing to work diligently. Now, God led her to the right field, but had she only stayed a short time, she would have left before Boaz arrived. God's will for her life could have potentially been missed if she was not willing to work hard. Does that mean that we, in our day and time, could miss out on God's will if we choose to be lazy rather than work our hardest? I believe it very well could. We live in an age where ease is overemphasized and laziness is one of the most coveted luxuries. But there is a reason it is said that idleness is the devil's workshop. I ask you, dear reader, to consider what ill things took place when someone was prolonging ease when they should have been working:

- **Lot** – He chose the well-watered plains of Sodom and Gomorrah, wishing to make life easy for him. This choice later

---

24. Ruth was the great-great-grandmother of Solomon.

led to several devastating things: the death of his wife, the death of two daughters and their husbands, and his other daughters conceiving the idea to get their father drunk and sleep with him so as to get pregnant. All of this came as of a result of living in the wicked atmosphere of Sodom.

- **Ish-bosheth** – He was sleeping in his bed at noon in the midst of a civil war.[25] He was easily murdered due to this (2 Samuel 4:1 – 7).

- **David** – When he should have been out with his army in the war against the Ammonites, he was lounging around his house in Jerusalem. Because of this, he caught Bath-sheba bathing and his adultery with her was committed shortly after (2 Samuel 11:1 – 4).

---

25. It is possible that Ish-bosheth simply went and took a small nap as opposed to have been in bed the entire morning. However, Baanah and Rechab were able to plan his murder while he laid in his bedchamber, so I feel that the passage leans more to the idea that Ish-bosheth had either been sleeping for a good length of time or that this was something he did rather habitually. Also note that this was in a time of civil war, so he certainly had things he should have been attending to.

Working hard is important and is a part of God's will for your life. If you neglect working diligently, you might actually miss what God has for you, just like Ruth could have missed Boaz if she decided to leave early. Now, this is not to say that rest is not important. I cannot stress the need for work without the great need to rest. I know too many people that work *too* hard and take no rest or breaks. Balance is crucial. God did not build us for constant, uninterrupted work. Relaxation and rest are very important in one's life. If you do not take time to rest, God will slap you with a mandatory break by way of exhaustion or sickness. Both extremes of not working at all or working too much are wrong. Work hard and rest well. Balancing these two aspects will be one of the healthiest things you can do for your life.

The first exchange between Ruth and Boaz:

"Then said Boaz unto Ruth, Hearest thou not, my daughter? Go not to glean in another field, neither go from hence, but abide here fast by my maidens: *Let* thine eyes *be* on the field that they do reap, and go thou after them: have I not charged the young men that they shall not touch thee? and when thou art athirst, go unto the vessels, and drink of *that* which the young men have drawn."

(Ruth 2:8 – 9)

There is much to expound upon here. First, Boaz told Ruth that she was not only welcome to his field, but encouraged to stay. I imagine this was monumental to Ruth, for she very easily could have received harsh and cruel treatment due to being a foreigner.

Secondly, he promised her protection. None of Boaz's men were allowed to touch her. Even if any of Boaz's servants did harbor any anger or wicked thoughts towards her, they were forbidden from acting on it. Acting against Boaz's orders would have meant sacrificing their occupation with him. It could have even meant sacrificing their reputation, for the rumor mill works twice as fast in small towns. Being dismissed from a wealthy man of integrity such as Boaz would have spread like wildfire and would have soiled a person's reputation with most, if not all, of the inhabitants of Bethlehem.

Thirdly, Boaz showed her an overabundance of kindness. Look closely where Boaz says "abide here fast by my maidens: *Let* thine eyes *be* on the field that they do reap, and go thou after them" and "when thou art athirst, go unto the vessels, and drink of *that* which the young men have drawn." Analyzing the former passage first, it is instructed in the Law that certain portions of the field were to be left for the poor: "thou shalt **leave** them for the poor and stranger:" (Leviticus 19:10). In order to be in accordance with the Law, all Boaz had to do was leave a portion of the crop so the poor could reap from there. With Ruth, however, he told her to stay next to his maidens. These maidens are believed to be employees of Boaz that would reap the bundles that the men would cut before them. Another belief is that these maidens were other poor/widows/strangers that were gleaning in Boaz's field since he actually followed the Law and because he was so kind. However, since Boaz frequently referred to them as "*my* maidens," I personally hold to the idea that they actually worked for Boaz. Regardless, Boaz was essentially giving Ruth the opportunity to not reap the leftovers, but part of the initial harvest itself. With the latter passage, he was telling Ruth that she could go and drink the water that his young men had drawn. This was water that was to be used for Boaz's workers as the harvest continued. Boaz was going above and beyond with Ruth, making her job far easier and giving her much more of his harvest than he was commanded to by the Law.

Ruth was overwhelmed by this. Boaz greatly exceeded her

expectations. In response, she gave him reverence by bowing

before him, asking why he bestowed such grace onto a stranger

like her. Boaz answered plainly: he was greatly moved and

impressed with Ruth's dedication to Naomi and her willingness to

forsake her homeland for Israel. Boaz knew that, logically

speaking, Ruth's decision to stick with Naomi didn't make sense.

Moreover, one thing that tends to be high on a woman's list of

needs is security. There was no guaranteed security leaving Moab.

There was no man to provide for her, but Ruth trusted in the God

of Israel to provide for her and that is exactly what He did via

Boaz. Boaz may not have been thinking that God was using him

to sufficiently provide for Ruth, but Boaz was eager to give Ruth

as much as he was able. This is further shown when he invited her

to eat with his workers. She was allowed all of the privileges that

they were, and Boaz personally delivered her food. The word

"reached" here is "צָבַט," (pronounced "tsaw-bat'") which means

"to hand out." Boaz very specifically gave her food himself.

Furthermore, note that Ruth "was sufficed, and left." These two words come from the Hebrew words "שָׂבַע שָׂבֵעַ," (pronounced "saw-bah', saw-bay'-ah") meaning "fill to satisfaction, to have enough, to satiate," and "יָתַר," (pronounced "yaw-thar'") meaning "to exceed, to excel, to cause to abound" respectively. Putting these together, it's saying that Ruth was able to eat until she was full and then she had food left over. I wonder how long it had been since she was able to be full like that.

Next, when Ruth went back to glean, Boaz commanded his workers to let her glean among the sheaves and even drop full handfuls for her. Here, we are told beyond a shadow of a doubt that Boaz was sacrificing part of his harvest for Ruth.[26] He did not suggest this, but ***commanded***. This is a big deal. He was a wealthy business owner, yet he was treating the lowest class of society with dignity and compassion. There is a moral to be found here that could be applied to us today. Just because someone is

---

26. Granted, Ruth was one person, just trying to get enough food for herself and Naomi. I am not saying that Ruth reaping part of the actual harvest would cost Boaz any high amount. The notion, however, is what is incredible, for we humans can be very stingy even when we have more than enough.

considered lower in the societal ladder doesn't mean they should be treated lesser. We are all people that are made in the image of God and everyone deserves compassion and respect.

Now, some question as to whether or not Boaz had ulterior motives in showing Ruth such treatment. And it's not wrong to speculate if he did or not. After all, Boaz was a single man and Ruth was new in town and without a husband. She was young and showed herself to be a hard worker. It would make sense for Boaz to want to impress her, especially if he found her attractive. So, let's analyze this. Did he do this with all of the poor? I personally don't believe so. I do think that he followed the Law for all of the poor, allowing them to glean as God commanded. I don't believe that he gave such ample attention and kindness to each poor individual, however. If he did, it could have been rather easy for people to take advantage of such graciousness and Boaz would not gain a decent harvest. Ergo, he would not have been a "mighty man of wealth."

Did he do this because he found Ruth attractive? Possibly. Many a man has done something nice for a beautiful woman. How many police officers have only given warnings to young, pretty women that clearly deserved a ticket? If anything, I believe her attractiveness may have been a factor, but was not the sole reason. Though, I must note that it does not say anywhere in the book of Ruth that Ruth was physically beautiful.[27] Please don't misunderstand, I'm not saying that she was ugly or hideous. However, the Bible does point out when a woman is exceptionally beautiful, such as with Rachel, Bath-sheba, Esther, and others. For Ruth, no description of beauty, fairness, or anything similar is mentioned. She was young, yes, but not necessarily noted as incredibly physically attractive. Again, I am not saying Ruth was ugly. She could have simply been average-looking. Take that how you will.

So, with a full observation, Ruth was a young, destitute widow that was a hard worker, but not necessarily very beautiful.

---

27. I say "physically" because she certainly had an inner beauty and virtue that outshone any outward beauty she could have had.

And, from previous passages that demonstrate Boaz's character, he was shown to be a wealthy older man of integrity that loved the Lord. Putting all of those pieces together, I don't believe Boaz had any ulterior motives, except one: Boaz knew that Naomi was a near kinsman to him. When the subject of the kinsman redeemer is brought up in 3:9 – 10, Boaz was not surprised at all. He had already made the connection when he found out Ruth was the daughter-in-law to Naomi. He knew that he could have been the kinsman redeemer to Ruth, so it is also believed that this overabundance of kindness was also due to him thinking "I need to provide for them because of my connection." But why provide for Ruth and Naomi this way and not just perform the part of the kinsman redeemer? Marrying Ruth would be a much more efficient way of ensuring Ruth and Naomi were taken care of. Why not, at the very least, bring it up to Ruth or discuss it with Naomi? Excellent questions. The answer is also found in Ruth 3:10, where it is made clear that Boaz assumed Ruth would want to marry a younger man. Boaz didn't entertain the idea that Ruth would be satisfied with marrying someone of his age. This further proves that Boaz was not a spring chicken. If Ruth was somewhere between her mid-twenties to early thirties, I wager Boaz could have been anywhere from his mid-forties to early fifties. Even in Bible times, that is a decent age gap. Furthermore, Boaz was already aware of a nearer kinsman that was to be the kinsman redeemer (Ruth 3:12), which is likely another reason he neglected to bring up the fact of who he was to Ruth.

Ruth had finally finished her long work day. Remember, this was all done in just one day, and in just that short amount of time Ruth worked, she was able to get a full ephah of barley. As stated earlier, an ephah was estimated to be between thirty and fifty pounds, which would have been an extraordinary amount for a widow woman gleaning in a field. The expectation for a widow woman gleaning would have been more around just one meal. Due to Ruth's diligence and Boaz's graciousness, Ruth was able to go home with far more than anyone expected, including Naomi. Now, Naomi's actual words are as follows: "Where hast thou gleaned to day? and where wroughtest thou? blessed be he that did take knowledge of thee," (Ruth 2:19) which is the older way of saying, "**GIRL**! Where have you **been** today??"

A little bit of hope seemed to be shining back into Naomi's life when she saw how much food Ruth was able to bring back. Naomi blessed the person who was so generous to Ruth before she even knew who it was, but she didn't have to wonder for long. Ruth immediately told her that the field owner was a man named Boaz. I can only imagine Naomi's initial reaction. In my mind, I see Naomi's mouth dropping slightly as her eyebrows shoot up. Then, as Ruth sits there, wondering why Naomi is reacting this way, Naomi's mind immediately starts turning in two different fashions:

1. Naomi realized, at least in some part, how God orchestrated both Ruth's and Boaz's steps to be at the perfect place at the perfect time for them to interact. The destitute widow and a wealthy near kinsman.

2. Naomi was undoubtedly piecing together how to get Boaz and Ruth to not only interact more, but to spark conversations of marriage between the two.

Most of that is conjecture, of course, but we do see Naomi quite different from her bitter self at the end of chapter one. She went from blaming the Lord at the end of chapter one to blessing the Lord at the end of chapter two. For God does show immeasurable kindness to all, though none of us deserve it. Furthermore, Naomi stated that the Lord was showing kindness to the living as well as the dead. This is to say that God was showing kindness to Naomi and Ruth (the living), but was also showing kindness to Elimelech, Mahlon, and Chilion (the dead) in the fashion that their name and line would not die off. By this declaration from Naomi, we know that she was already planning out a wedding for Ruth and Boaz and was even expecting grandchildren soon. Ruth, possibly still in confusion at Naomi's sudden excitement and blessing to the Lord, received a small explanation from Naomi that Boaz was a near kinsman to them. I cannot say whether or not Ruth understood what that meant, for it is unclear if the principle of the near kinsman was a part of Moabite culture. I doubt it was, but cannot say for sure. Of course, Ruth might have known due to Naomi teaching her about the Law. That, or Ruth may have still been completely in the dark and did not understand why Boaz being a near kinsman was such delightful news. Perhaps Naomi intended that and wished for Ruth and Boaz to fall in love naturally rather than forcing it.

Whatever Naomi's mind or intentions, she strictly instructed Ruth to stay by Boaz's maidens when Ruth mentioned that she was going to work alongside Boaz's young men. Hearing of Boaz's generosity and likely knowing Boaz's character, Naomi knew that no man would be better for Ruth than Boaz. She did not want to risk Ruth getting interested in any other man or have any other man getting interested in her. Naomi further instructed that Ruth not go to any other field besides Boaz's. Naomi was trusting that God was working something out and put in her own efforts to ensure the matchmaking stayed on track. Moreover, Ruth, being the obedient daughter-in-law that she was, followed all of Naomi's instructions without question. Whether she understood Naomi's intentions or not, we are not told. I like to think that Ruth had no idea why and was simply doing what she was told. Such obedience is how we ought to follow God's leading, knowing that He knows best and has the best in mind for us.

In the very last sentence of chapter two, we see that Ruth was following Naomi's orders to stick by Boaz's maidens as she gleaned from Boaz's field. However, it is important to note that Ruth did this from the end of the barley harvest and into the wheat harvest. Barley harvest supposedly took place in late March or April, while wheat harvest supposedly took place anywhere from late April to June. Assuming Ruth and Boaz met at the very beginning of the barely harvest, they could have been seeing each other in the field for up to three months now. However, it would seem that throughout all this time, no romance had sparked between the two. Of course, by our standards, three months sounds extremely short for love to blossom (depending on who you talk to), however this wasn't entirely about love. Rather, Naomi was likely waiting for Boaz to go forward with his responsibilities as a near kinsman. At this point, Naomi may have been wondering what was taking Boaz so long to start speaking to Ruth or even herself about his kinsman redeemer obligations. Boaz had his reasons for not going forward with those obligations, some of which we have already spoken on and others that we will touch on later. The most significant (and one that Naomi may not have realized) being that there was a nearer kinsman.

Regardless, Naomi believed a more direct approach was needed at this point. Whether or not she thoroughly discussed the concept of the kinsman redeemer with Ruth prior to this point, Naomi seemed to have talked it over with Ruth now. Seeing as how Naomi began the conversation, it would seem that she felt it might have been an uncomfortable subject for Ruth:

"Then Naomi her mother in law said unto her, My daughter, shall I not seek rest for thee, that it may be well with thee?"
(Ruth 3:1)

This is my perception of it, but it sounds like Naomi was beginning this conversation as gently as possible, trying to hone in on the benefits of Ruth marrying Boaz. Gingerly urging Ruth to focus on those rather than the potential objections Ruth might have against such an arrangement. This further makes me believe that, up to this point, Ruth did not know Naomi's intentions concerning Boaz. We know that Ruth knew Boaz to be very generous and kind, but Ruth could have very well still been in mourning for her late husband, Mahlon. After all, in chapter one, the text conveys the feeling that Naomi decided to go back from Moab to Israel very shortly after Mahlon and Chilion's death. For all we know, it could have only been a few months since Ruth's husband passed, which would make perfect sense as to why the discussion of a new marriage would be a touchy subject.

Whether or not it was a sensitive subject, Naomi unfolded her plan to Ruth by telling her that Boaz was going to be busy with processing the rest of the barley harvest that night. The term "winnoweth" is used, which comes from the Hebrew word "זָרָה" (pronounced "zaw-raw'"). This word means "to toss," which shows us that "winnoweth" can be likened to threshing, which made perfect sense since Boaz was at a threshing floor. We can also learn from this that, though the apparent time frame for the wheat harvest was from late April to June, it was evidently not too long after the barley harvest. We can observe this due to the barley not being completely processed and being used for food yet. Then again, they did not have the kind of efficient machinery that we do nowadays and it might have simply taken them longer to finish everything. Admittedly, I am no farmer and I urge you to study it out for yourself. At the end of the day, however, whether it was earlier or later, it makes little difference. The point was that Naomi knew where Boaz would be that night and was instructing Ruth to go there.

Beginning her very specific instructions, Naomi told Ruth to wash and "put thy upon raiment thee." This feels a bit unnecessary to add. Of course Ruth shouldn't go without clothes. However, rather than meaning simply to put on clothes, I believe this is pointing to the idea that Ruth was still wearing her mourning apparel. Remember, Mahlon could have passed away only several months ago. Moreover, if Ruth was wearing her mourning garments, this would be all the more reason for Boaz not to approach her with the idea of the kinsman redeemer. He was respecting the loss of Mahlon without trying to intrude with the idea that Ruth ought to remarry right away.

Moving on, Naomi further instructed Ruth to get down to the threshing floor and stay hidden until Boaz laid down to sleep. Then she was to "uncover his feet," and lie down at his feet. There are many speculations as to whether or not this was simply cultural or if it dealt more with seductive tactics. I lean towards the idea that it was strictly cultural and demonstrated humility. After all, what was Ruth doing? She was essentially proposing to Boaz. Of course, not in the same way that most people do today. This proposal of marriage was not based on romance, but based in God's law and out of need for Ruth's well-being and the continuation of Elimelech's line. All the same, she proposed to Boaz. In America, it's customary for a man to get down on one knee when proposing. Though it may be done more out of tradition in our day and age, it was a gesture to demonstrate humility and respect when asking for a woman's hand in marriage. For Ruth, she wasn't simply kneeling, but lying completely down at the base of Boaz's feet. The lower someone got to the ground, the more humility and respect they showed to that individual.[28] Since Ruth was lying completely on the ground, she wished to convey the utmost respect and humility towards Boaz when she brought forth this request and Boaz would have recognized that (once he woke up enough).

If anything was done crudely or improperly, the fault lies on Naomi, for she was the one who instructed Ruth to do these things. Ruth, being so devoted to Naomi and possibly still unfamiliar with Israeli customs, would have followed without question. It's not outside the realm of possibility that Naomi would do something less than godly in this case, for we have seen her with a wrong attitude towards God before. As for the explanation for what was done, Naomi first told Ruth to make herself known only to Boaz. This was likely for the day and time

---

28. This is also a great place to point out that worship always requires bowing for this very reason. Contrary to what many people think today, worship isn't waving one's hands in the air, but going down to the floor in reverence.

in which they lived. Not everyone was as godly as Boaz. Others would have likely run her off, suspecting her to try and steal from the harvest. Secondly, it was to be a private meeting with no one else around. We can assume that this, at least in part, was to not bring about such a revelation of Boaz's responsibility with the pressure of others hearing it as well. It could have brought embarrassment or even influenced Boaz's decision to not go through with it (this is from Naomi's thinking. Boaz would have likely accepted even if others were around). Furthermore, Naomi told her to do all of this knowing that both parties had upright character. She wouldn't have encouraged Ruth in this way if Boaz was a man given to lustful appetites. She cared deeply for her daughter-in-law and wouldn't have endangered her so. It should also be made aware that the verses speaking about Boaz drinking do not imply alcohol. He had been working for many hours in the hot sun. The obvious drink he would have consumed would be water. He was not merry due to intoxication, but the harvest was a time of celebration. He would have been happy at the bounty brought in from the harvest and glad the work was completed. Now he could rest.

So, upon being awoken around midnight by either a dream or some noise that stirred him, he finally spotted Ruth. Being just woken up and likely not fully comprehending everything, combined with the fact that it was dark, Boaz did not recognize Ruth. All he knew is that a woman was lying at his feet. His mind was probably reeling. Was this a thief come to steal from his harvest? He questioned her, asking who she was, to which she answered "I *am* Ruth thine handmaid: spread therefore thy skirt over thine handmaid; for thou *art* a near kinsman" (Ruth 3:9). The phrase "spread therefore thy skirt over thine handmaid" reflected what Boaz himself had said to Ruth back in 2:12 when he said "under whose wings thou art come to trust." Both phrases use the Hebrew word "כָּנָף," (pronounced "kaw-nawf") which means "edge or extremity." When Boaz had stated it, he was referring to God's wings of protection. When Ruth stated it, she was referring to Boaz's skirt of protection. Ruth was using Boaz's own wording to essentially say "You said before that I have come under God's protection and care. God has now appointed you to be His protection and care for me."

Boaz's fears were calmed as he realized it was only Ruth, but now he was given something else entirely to think about. Ruth had just invoked the kinsman redeemer. Ruth was asking Boaz to marry her. Boaz's immediate response is one that we all had wished to hear, especially Ruth:

"And he said, Blessed *be* **thou of the LORD, my daughter:** *for* **thou hast shewed more kindness in the latter end than at the beginning, inasmuch as thou followedst not young men, whether poor or rich. And now, my daughter, fear not; I will do to thee all that thou requirest: for all the city of my people doth know that thou** *art* **a virtuous woman."**

(Ruth 3:10 – 11)

A positive response, showing us that Boaz was very pleased by this request. He stated that Ruth showed more kindness in the latter end than in the beginning. So what is the kindness that Ruth showed at the beginning? The only one that Boaz specifically spoke of was the following:

"And Boaz answered and said unto her, It hath fully been shewed me, all that thou hast done unto thy mother in law since the death of thine husband: and *how* thou hast left thy father and thy mother, and the land of thy nativity, and art come unto a people which thou knewest not heretofore."

(Ruth 2:11)

So how was Ruth's proposal for marriage considered more kindness than taking care of Naomi? It could be considered a greater kindness because she forsook her home and family for Naomi. Now, in Boaz's mind, she was forsaking her own desires for the husband she wanted. She was doing this for the sake of Elimelech's name and Mahlon's name rather than going after a younger man or a richer man.[29] This goes to show that Boaz thought very little of himself. The age gap between them probably

---

29. Though Boaz himself was a very wealthy man.

added to his poor reflection of himself. He did not even consider the idea that he was desirable to her, but felt that she was doing this out of obligation only. I tend to think that Ruth had great fondness for Boaz at this point after he showed her such compassion and respect throughout the time they knew one another. Of course, the Bible does not specifically speak on this point.

Another point that needs to be made is that Boaz stated Ruth was known not only by him to be a virtuous woman, but all of Bethlehem. Had any of her actions been done with seduction or promiscuity in mind, she would not have been called virtuous in this instance. Furthermore, the Bible does not hint that anything sexual took place. If something of that nature had taken place, it would likely have been noted. The Bible does not flatter its heroes.

After the happy proclamation from Boaz, however, one sour note resounds:

"And now it is true that I *am thy* near kinsman: howbeit there is a kinsman nearer than I. Tarry this night, and it shall be in the morning, *that* if he will perform unto thee the part of a kinsman, well; let him do the kinsman's part: but if he will not do the part of a kinsman to thee, then will I do the part of a kinsman to thee, *as* the LORD liveth: lie down until the morning."

(Ruth 3:12 – 13)

Still a favorable answer. Boaz was promising that Ruth would indeed have a kinsman redeemer one way or another. Boaz was not the closest kinsman, but he would alert the closer kinsman of his duties. If the nearest kinsman would not do his part, then Boaz would. Still a favorable answer, but not the answer Ruth probably wanted to hear. The Bible sadly does not give us much of Ruth's thoughts or opinions throughout the book, but I tend to think that Ruth was upset by this update. She had been given ample amounts of time to get to know Boaz. He treated her with respect, kindness, charity, and he loved the Lord. He had already demonstrated, without attempting to pursue Ruth, that he was a very upstanding man to marry. Both Ruth and Naomi knew that Ruth would have been taken care of and treated well should she have married Boaz. But now, another person was brought into the picture. A man Ruth knew nothing about. Was he just as good as Boaz? Was he worse? Was he wealthy enough to care for both Ruth and Naomi? Was he already married? So many questions must have burned in Ruth's heart at the revelation that Boaz was not the nearest kinsman. All the same, she said nothing. She only followed Boaz's instructions to lie down and get some rest.

Ruth 3:14 – 18

Ruth stayed the night, lying at Boaz's feet. This passage has been the speculation of many Bible readers as to if this was inappropriate conduct or not between two single people. First and foremost, it is never wise for two unmarried people of different genders to be alone together. Especially if they're attracted to each other. Ruth and Boaz arguably fit all of those. However, both had the character and respect for each other to refrain from youthful lusts. That is not to say that this was right simply because they had character. Any person of character can fall to sin in a moment of weakness when given opportunity.

Ruth and Boaz's actions in this passage are not to be purposely replicated, but that is not to say that there were not valid reasons for them. For Boaz was not asking Ruth to stay because he desired her company, but for her own safety. It was midnight in the time of the judges. Terrible things could have happened to Ruth if she ventured out at night. Instead, at Boaz's orders, she left in the very early morning before anyone else woke up so as to avoid any other problematic encounters. If anyone had known she had been sleeping at Boaz's feet, accusations of fornication could have taken place and it would have shamed both Boaz's name as well as Ruth's. However, Boaz would not let her leave without giving her six measures of barley so as to ensure Ruth and Naomi had enough to eat.

Upon getting back to Naomi, Naomi was ready with questions as to how everything had gone. We aren't sure how long Naomi thought the whole encounter should have taken, whether it should have been a relatively short conversation or taken the entire night. Seeing that Ruth had left the day before and hadn't returned until the early morning (and with Boaz's gift of barley), Naomi was likely hopeful that Ruth had not been rejected. A simple rejection would have taken very little time for Ruth to be dismissed and for her to return to Naomi. And so, once Ruth arrived, Naomi summarized all of her questions into one:

"And when she came to her mother in law, she said, Who *art* thou, my daughter?"

(Ruth 3:16a)

It wasn't that Naomi was unsure of who Ruth was, but was asking her if she was now, in a manner of speaking, Mrs. Boaz. Naomi was asking if the proposal had been answered with a "yes." Ruth, in turn, told her all of what happened. Ending the story with the fact that Boaz had given her the six measures of barley, Naomi comforted Ruth with assurance of Boaz's character:

"Then said she, Sit still, my daughter, until thou know how the matter will fall: for the man will not be in rest, until he have finished the thing this day."

(Ruth 3:18)

Naomi trusted Boaz's integrity so much, she knew, without a doubt, that he would work relentlessly until the matter of Ruth's kinsman redeemer was accomplished. Since Boaz is obviously a picture of Jesus Christ, we can also rest at ease when we take our requests and needs before the Lord. For the Lord is never at rest, always endcavoring to provide for us in the way that is best for us. Not always in the way that *we* think is best, but in the way that He knows is best.

The gate of the city. In this culture, it was customary to hold all official business in the city gate. It is believed by some for Boaz himself to have been an elder of Bethlehem, especially with how he seats himself in the gate with a sense of authority and familiarity. Being both a mighty man of wealth and a godly man of character, it would make sense for him to be an elder in the gate. However, the Bible does not explicitly say. Elder or not, he found himself a place in the gate and waited for the closest kinsman to arrive.

The closest kinsman arrived and was hailed by Boaz. The first unsettling thing we notice about this individual is that he is not named at all in the book of Ruth. It is almost as if he wished to be left anonymous and not at all affiliated with the account of Ruth so as to withhold further association with the Moabitess. That, or I could see him being left unnamed in the Bible as a form of shame due to his unwillingness to perform his responsibilities as the kinsman redeemer. Regardless, the meeting was set and ten elders were gathered as witnesses to this official family business. Boaz explained Naomi's situation concisely and that Elimelech's land was being sold. If the specific legalities or details in how this kind of transaction works are listed in Scripture, it is not found in the book of Ruth. I assume something like this would be found in the Pentateuch, but must be candid in that I am not sure if it is mentioned at all. In this account, it seems to be taken for granted that the readers are fully aware of how this works, whether it was mortgaged during the famine to buy food and Naomi was going to gift it to the nearest kinsman after he redeemed it out of debt, or some other form. Boaz was giving the nearest kinsman legal notice so that, if he refused, the opportunity would fall to the next nearest kinsman, which was Boaz.

However, Boaz initially left out a crucial detail when it came to the purchase of the land: Ruth. And since he did, the nearest kinsman seemed rather charmed at the idea of taking Elimelech's land. He informed Boaz that he would buy it. Upon that, Boaz added that Mahlon's widow would also require a kinsman redeemer to raise up children to Mahlon's name. At this point, the nearest kinsman said the following:

"And the kinsman said, I cannot redeem *it* for myself, lest I mar mine own inheritance: redeem thou my right to thyself; for I cannot redeem *it.*"

(Ruth 4:6)

Now, how would marrying Ruth mar his inheritance? There are a few possible explanations:

1. Marrying a Moabite woman would cause him to lose his inheritance from his father. Essentially saying that his father would not allow him to marry a non-Israelite woman and still receive the inheritance he was due after his father's passing.

2.	Buying the land from Naomi and providing for two widows (one of which he was supposed to sire at least one child with) would cause him to spend all of his inheritance so he would have nothing left afterwards.

3.	The nearest kinsman did not want to take a Moabite woman to wife and came up with a valid-sounding excuse.

4.	The nearest kinsman was already married and did not want Jacob-level family drama and jealousy.[30]

Ultimately, we are not told the exact reason, so it is left up to conjecture. The point was that the nearest kinsman would not buy it, so he drew off his shoe and gave it to Boaz. Now, why was this a custom? In verse 7, it is noted that this was done when concerning "redeeming and changing." "Redeeming" would be referring to this very act we are seeing in the book of Ruth, that being the actions of the kinsman redeemer. The word "changing,"

---

30. If it did happen to be this one, I feel we can hardly judge him. That is a very valid reason. Especially when Boaz was single, willing, and wealthy.

however, is more peculiar. Looking up the Hebrew word for it, which would be "תְּמוּרָה," (pronounced "*tem-oo-raw*") it deals with bartering, restitution, exchanging, and recompensing. But why taking off one's shoe? I believe the action has a two-fold purpose. The first being simply proof that the transaction was done, but the latter being more symbolic. The one who was giving up his shoe was symbolically giving up any right he previously had of walking on the land after the transaction was done. There was a third consideration that was brought up by some that he would have to walk abnormally, wearing only one shoe, as a shame unto him for not doing his responsibilities. I could see that being valid in the case of the kinsman redeemer, but the passage clearly states that this was also done with normal bartering and wouldn't make sense for someone to be shamed for only completing ordinary, every-day business.

After completing the business affairs with the unnamed kinsman, Boaz ensured everything was concluded properly by very clearing stating before the witnesses gathered that the unnamed kinsman had given up his right to the land and was neglecting his responsibilities concerning Ruth.

Though some would consider the language Boaz used crude when it came to him saying that he had "purchased" Ruth, one must consider that he was speaking according to the business-oriented ordeal that had been taking place. Boaz was making certain that the witnesses before him understood that Ruth was legally and rightfully his wife now. If the dealings had been vague to the witnesses, accusations of fornication could have arisen between Boaz and Ruth. Boaz, being a godly man and caring deeply for Ruth's testimony, wanted to prevent anything of the sort to ever take place. Furthermore, in the original Hebrew, it sounds far less like Boaz claimed he had "purchased" Ruth. The

Hebrew word is "קָנָה," (pronounced "*kaw-naw*") which can be translated "to own" with the sense of being jealous over. Boaz was essentially saying that Ruth was now his to be jealous over. And, contrary to popular belief, jealousy is not inherently evil.[31] It is actually inherently a good thing. It is innate to every couple because there is an understanding, at a subconscious level, that your wife/husband belongs to you, just as much as you belong to your husband/wife. Your spouse is not to be romantically shared, but to be exclusively yours. When this is not followed, trouble always brews. Look at the instance of Jacob and his four wives, or Elkanah and his two wives. Unrest, division, and heartache are always born out of situations where exclusive faithfulness is not adhered to.

---

31. Jealousy, when it goes to the extreme, can be a major issue. Just as anything taken to the extreme can. Jealousy is right in its place and is not meant to consume someone when no one has done anything wrong. Part of what makes a relationship healthy is trusting your partner to be faithful. Simply seeing them speak with or spend time with another member of the opposite gender from time to time is not a legitimate cause for getting riled up and feverishly jealous.

Back to the passage, the witnesses demonstrated that they understood what took place and agreed in their part of being observers of it. In the legal sense, if Ruth and Boaz's marriage ever came into question, these witnesses could be called upon to testify that it was indeed valid and done lawfully.

Lastly, before the meeting was officially finished, the witnesses gave forth blessings to Boaz's marriage. It was only fitting since there was about to be a wedding. Moreover, Boaz is believed to have been a single man his entire life up until this point and, as we have established before, he was not necessarily young. Some may have thought he would never marry, so this was certainly time to give a celebratory blessing. There are three blessings given in total:

1. For Ruth to be like Rachel and like Leah. The witnesses were not saying that Ruth ought to be like them in character or in like circumstance, but to be fruitful as they were. Leah gave birth to seven children. Rachel gave birth to two. And

those children all became great with their own lineages as the tribes of Israel.

2. For Boaz to do worthily and become famous in Bethlehem. Now, Boaz was already doing worthily and he was already famous in Bethlehem. I would wager the idea behind this blessing was that they were saying that he *continue* to do worthily and be famous or to increase in those factors.

3. For both Ruth and Boaz to be like the house of Pharez that was born from Tamar and Judah. Thankfully, again, the witnesses were not referring to the situation behind the relationship, Judah being Tamar's father-in-law (Genesis 38), but the strength and size of the lineage. The tribe of Judah, from Pharez, multiplied exceedingly. In Numbers 26:21, the tribe of Judah was numbered at 76,500, the largest tribe of Israel. Many of the other tribes at that point are significantly lesser, the closest being Isaachar at 66,300.

The passage jumps forward slightly and begins tying up the ends of this account, the author beginning to summarize more rather than retell the story with each particular step. Ruth and Boaz were married. And though the passage is now written in a more summary type fashion, it does seem to imply that Ruth became pregnant straight away. If that is how it took place, many would argue that there was nothing physically wrong with Ruth when she was married to Mahlon, but fruit of the womb was likely withheld due to Mahlon's disobedience.[32]

At Obed's birth, Naomi returns as a focus in the account, being blessed by women of Bethlehem. What a stark contrast we find from the Naomi of the end of chapter one. She was empty at the end of chapter one, but now is found restored by the end of chapter four. Provided for once again by her daughter-in-law's new husband and no longer in poverty. Even more wonderful, she

---

32. It could also be that Mahlon's perceived ill state was a factor, but much of that is straying into conjecture.

was finally made a grandmother. Though she was not the biological grandmother, she had been found in Ruth's eyes as more worthy of the title "mother" than the woman who had given birth to Ruth, else Ruth would have likely stayed in Moab. So though the semantics dictated that Naomi was not related to this child, Ruth and the other women of Bethlehem shooed them away from their minds. After all, Naomi became Obed's "nurse," which did not refer to her as giving the child breast-milk, but was rather one who became like a second mother to Obed. Such are most grandparents who adore their children's little ones.

The blessing from the women of Bethlehem all came to pass. Obed's name would indeed become famous in Israel. His name would be recorded in the sacred Scriptures to this day. He would be known as the grandfather of David, the greatest earthly king in Israel's history. As we see with how Naomi loved the child, he surely became a restorer of Naomi's life and nourished her in her old age. Lastly, the blessing shifted to Ruth, for none of these wonderful things would have come to pass had Ruth given up on Naomi. Ruth had stayed faithfully by Naomi's side, loving her selflessly and doing her best to provide for Naomi. Ruth was indeed better to Naomi than seven sons. She had served her mother-in-law to the utmost degree and the Lord used that to bring all of the wonderful things in this book to pass. Possibly connecting those dots as well, the child was named Obed. Obed means "serving," likely referring to the fact that Ruth never stopped serving Naomi.

The lineage of Obed is given at the end of the book. The lineage of Ruth and Boaz eventually leading to David. This shows us that Ruth, a Moabitess, was not only now a part of the royal line of Israel, but she was ushered into the line of the Messiah. What an honor for a woman who firmly chose to follow the God of Israel rather than the gods of her home country.

As for Obed, he was to be named under Mahlon's name, but strangely enough, Obed is consistently referred to as Boaz's son throughout the Bible. This can be found in 1 Chronicles 2:11 – 12, Matthew 1:5, and Luke 3:32. I must disclose that I am not certain of why it was done this way, but can only guess:

1. Mahlon, perceived to have been judged by the Lord with his death,[33] was found ill-fitting to be considered in the line of the Messiah due to his disobedience.

---

33. Just to reiterate, Scripture does not confirm that he was judged by the Lord with his death, though it is a possibility.

2.   The Bible was simply being true to Obed's biological father. Though Mahlon may have been considered Obed's father in Obed's life, he was recorded under his true parentage in the holy Scriptures so as to not seem as if the Bible was putting forth a lie.

There are possibly others, but those are the pertinent two that I can think of. Moving on, there is a wonderful picture that is shown throughout this book that I have not yet touched on thoroughly. Throughout Ruth's account, we can see that Boaz pictures Jesus, Naomi pictures the Holy Spirit, and Ruth pictures the lost. Ruth was a destitute foreigner that followed Naomi from the land of heathen Moab to the promised land of Israel. Though she could provide herself a few meals by gleaning, Ruth had no way of living abundantly in a society where men were the only ones who could conduct business. She could not even keep her own land. She was destined for a hard and miserable existence. But Boaz showed her grace when Ruth could offer him nothing in return. He invited her to stay in his field rather than wander about to other fields. He gave her above and beyond that which she expected. Then, when urged by Naomi, Ruth asked to be redeemed as his own wife and Boaz happily obliged.

Now, take that and apply the pictures to them. The lost are wandering through life, able to provide themselves some fleeting happiness, but always missing something. Not able to live abundantly in God's purpose. Their lives are destined to be hard and miserable until death claims them and they are swallowed into the bowels of hell. But Jesus has shown all of humanity grace by providing salvation by His death on the cross. He did this when we could offer Him nothing in return. All of our righteousnesses are as filthy rags (Isaiah 64:6) and we were stuck in the mire of our sin. But the Holy Spirit urges us to follow His leading directly to Jesus. For Jesus offers us our only escape from the darkness of hell and providing our every need in life. And once we follow the prompting of the Holy Spirit and asked to be redeem by the Saviour, He happily obliges. The picture is so clear. I would advise you, dear reader, to go back through the book of Ruth again with these thoughts in mind as you read it. Now, granted, it's not a perfect resemblance. Naomi certainly falls short for always picturing the Holy Spirit, as does Boaz for Jesus. The thing is, however, that it's not supposed to be perfect because it's a true, historical account of real people and no one is going to picture Jesus or the Holy Spirit perfectly aside from Jesus and the Holy Spirit.

In my final thoughts, there are some other points I would like discuss before the closing of this commentary. Ruth and Boaz's relationship has been the focus of many marital sermons and conversations. Now, why is that? We hardly saw their married life. From 4:13 to the end of the chapter shows them as a married couple and most of the focus was on Obed and Naomi during that passage. This is true, but Ruth and Boaz's relationship, although not romantic at first, began all the way back in 2:5. And what do we see there? Boaz showed Ruth compassion and Ruth showed Boaz honor. In a marriage relationship, love is a woman's greatest need and respect is a man's greatest need. They really started off on the right foot. Furthermore, as their relationship continued, they persisted in showing each other reverence and kindness. They even had this sense that the other person was more deserving, more wonderful, and more praiseworthy than themselves. Lastly, they followed what was biblical concerning their relationship as it swung from platonic to romantic.

All of that is the key to a healthy marriage. If you're a husband, you need to show your wife love. If you're a wife, you need to show your husband respect. Do that and your spouse will be encouraged to show you what you need. I can't count how many times I've wanted to do something special for my wife when she simply made me feel like the man of the house. Now, I *am* the man of my house, but it makes it all the more wonderful when she makes me *feel* that way. Likewise, my wife seeks to honor me after I demonstrate my love for her. It's a beautiful cycle that only makes our marriage thrive.

Secondly, we all need to keep our view of our spouses in check. Belittling or looking down on your husband/wife, even subconsciously, will cause coldness to come into your marriage. And, if prolonged enough, it will cause the relationship to wither and die. Boaz looked at Ruth like she was more exceptional than he was. Ruth did likewise. Now, to be clear, balance is key. I am not advocating that wives ought to worship their husbands as a god or vice versa. Nor am I saying that people ought to think of themselves as worthless. But people often state that they married their better half. Putting each other up on a pedestal will certainly not hurt your relationship at all.

Lastly, and most importantly, make sure that you follow the Bible concerning your marriage. Showing love and respect is good. Putting your spouse on a pedestal is also good. But if we are going to be the kind of couples God has in mind for us to be, we need to be biblical. Ruth and Boaz would have never come together had they not followed what the Law stated concerning the kinsman redeemer. And you and your spouse will not come to the culmination of what God wishes for you if you are not willing to follow His plan in the Bible. That means that couples ought to first read their Bibles. Preferably together, but I understand that it doesn't always work out that way. After reading it, follow it. Pray together and pray for each other. These are the keys to a strong, godly marriage. For we cannot put our spouse as our focus in life. We must put Jesus as our focus. If both the husband and wife run towards Jesus, they will in turn grow closer and closer together.

Please leave an honest review on Amazon or send it

to krohnstories@gmail.com.

Every review helps and is appreciated!

Note to the Reader

Dear Reader,

Though this is a KJV Bible commentary that you are reading, I feel that it doesn't hurt to explain the plan of salvation at every opportunity I am given. What I am about to tell you does not come from a heart that is holier-than-thou or just wanting you to join my church. I tell you this because I am concerned for your soul. It's similar to a man at a beach that sees a shark in the water. Some of those who are swimming in the ocean don't notice the danger. So what should he do? Make them aware of the danger by yelling "SHARK!" And that's what I'm endeavoring to do. I want to warn you of the danger that's coming at the end of your life.

Recently, there have been a decent amount of people I have known that suddenly passed away. Most were unexpected and very shocking. It reminded me of a rather depressing truth: death is coming for all of us. We don't know when and we don't know how, but death will eventually come. And, for some, I kept thinking to myself "Where are they now?" I didn't know some of their faiths or beliefs. But I believe in a God that made the heavens and the earth. I believe that, in the beginning, the world was perfect. I believe that mankind sinned against God, thus shattering the perfection of creation. I believe that all have sinned and are worthy of judgment. I believe that Jesus Christ, God in human flesh, lived a sinless life and died on the cross so He might pay the price of our sin for us. I believe that anyone who calls upon Him will be saved from a literal, eternal hell. And I, as one of His believers, am to go out and tell others of His salvation so that they can be saved as well.

In today's age, there are thousands of faiths that someone can believe in. And people flock to religions because we, as humanity, have an inner knowledge that there is something bigger than all of us that first brought everything into being. Even atheists know that a higher being exists out there. They just choose to reject it. When my friends died, it forced me to think of their eternal destination. Their opportunity to choose is past and they are either in heaven with the Lord, or burning in the penetrating darkness of hell. This is not the most cheery stuff, I admit. But, as I said earlier, I'm concerned for your eternal destination. And I don't want anyone to go to hell. I wouldn't wish that on my worst enemy. So, if you'll permit me, I'd like to tell you about how you can get away from the shark, so to speak. Now, before I get into it, I will let you know that I'm not trying to make you my disciple or anything. I'm not trying to get accolades for converting someone to Christianity, and I'm most certainly not trying to force you become a Christian against your will. No, I'm telling you about it so you can make the choice for yourself. From my perspective, people are in grave danger. And, again, we don't know when our life will end. So what kind of person would I be if I believed in a real place called hell, but never told anyone how to be rescued from it?

So, without further ado, I'd like to lay out the steps of salvation, if that's all right with you.

1. <u>God is holy and cannot be in the presence of sin.</u>

"For I am the LORD that bringeth you up out of the land of
Egypt, to be your God: ye shall therefore be holy, for I am holy."

Leviticus 11:45

"There is none holy as the LORD: for there is none beside Thee:
neither is there any rock like our God."

1 Samuel 2:2

"Holy, holy, holy, Lord God Almighty, which was, and is, and is
to come."

Revelation 4:8b

Holy is a word that means "set apart," "morally blameless,"
or "sacred". Essentially, it means to be without sin. Since God is
holy, associating with sin would nullify His holiness. It's like
mixing oil with water or trying to put light and darkness together.
It can't happen. If God and humanity are going to be in each

other's presence, one of them needs to change. And it's not going to be God.

2. <u>Every human is a sinner. Even the tiniest sin makes you incapable of being in God's presence and worthy of His wrath.</u>

"For all have sinned, and come short of the glory of God;"

Romans 3:23

This is where some believe that they are "good enough" with God because they haven't committed the big sins like murder, rape, etc., but if you think that, just look at the Ten Commandments and ask yourself "Have I broken any of these?":

1. Thou shalt have no other gods before Me.

2. Thou shalt not make unto thee any graven image.

3. Thou shalt not take the name of the LORD thy God in vain.

4. Remember the sabbath to keep it holy.

5. Honor thy father and mother.

6. Thou shalt not kill.

7. Thou shalt not commit adultery.

8. Thou shalt not steal.

9. Thou shalt not bear false witness.

10. Thou shalt not covet.

People usually acknowledge that they've broken at least one of the Ten Commandments (usually the one that deals with lying, at least). But, in the New Testament, Jesus added a higher standard with a few of these commandments. He said that if you held anger in your heart towards someone, you've committed murder in your heart. He also said if you look upon someone with lust who is not your spouse, you're committing mental adultery (adultery here is actually referring to sexual sin in general, not necessarily the specific act of cheating on a spouse, though that is included). Now, most people have done those things as well, which makes them lying, murdering adulterers. And that's just three of the Ten Commandments. But even if someone had only broken one little aspect of God's law, the New Testament also says this:

"For whosoever shall keep the whole law, and yet offend in one

point, he is guilty of all."

James 2:10

It's like having a string tied to a ball. The string has ten

knots in it, representing the Ten Commandments. If someone were

to cut the knots with scissors, how many would they have to cut

before the ball hits the ground? Just one. The same is true with

God's law. If you just broke only one part of it, you're guilty.

You're a sinner. And you cannot be in His presence. Thankfully,

that's not where it ends.

3. Sin leads to spiritual death, but Christ leads to spiritual life. The

spiritual death will separate sinners from God to eternal hell. But

Jesus paid the penalty so we can go to heaven.

"But God commendeth His love toward us, in that, while we were

yet sinners, Christ died for us."

Romans 5:8

"For the wages of sin is death; but the gift of God is eternal life through Jesus Christ our Lord."

Romans 6:23

A price needed to be paid because of humanity's sin. It can be likened to someone committing a crime of property damage. Someone has to pay for to repair the damage. But let's say it wasn't just any property that was damaged. Say it was something incredibly valuable, like the Eiffel Tower. If someone destroyed the Eiffel Tower, that would probably cost millions of dollars to replace. A price that most people cannot pay. When it comes to sin, the cost was even higher. Humanity in of itself could not pay for the cost of redemption. We needed someone to pay the debt for us. That someone is Jesus Christ. He paid the price by being a sacrifice for humanity. He is God, which means He is perfect and able to pay the cost for sin. But He is also man, because only a man could redeem mankind. His innocent blood was shed in order to give everyone an opportunity to be forgiven of their debt.

4. <u>Repent and place faith in Jesus. Believe that Jesus is the Son of God and claim the gift of eternal salvation that He offers you freely.</u>

"For God so loved the world, that He gave His only begotten Son, that whosoever believeth in Him should not perish, but have everlasting life."

John 3:16

"Repent ye therefore, and be converted, that your sins may be blotted out, when the times of refreshing shall come from the presence of the Lord;"

Acts 3:19.

"That if thou shalt confess with thy mouth the Lord Jesus, and shalt believe in thine heart that God hath raised Him from the dead, thou shalt be saved."

Romans 10:9

This sounds too simple to a lot of people. But Jesus already did all of the work for us. All we need to do is accept the gift. Imagine that we are all on death row, but a pardon has been offered to everyone. All we need to do is accept the pardon and we're set free. But we have the choice to also refuse the pardon. In history, there have been people placed on death row that were given a pardon from the president, yet they refused and were put to death anyway. The same is true for spiritual salvation. You can refuse it. But the consequence is eternal hell.

Again, I want to make it crystal clear that I'm not trying to force any of this upon you. I'm simply telling you this because I believe it to be true and I don't want you to suffer a terrible fate of going to hell when you die. Now, I realize that this is not always what people want to hear, but you must understand my motives and that they are not malicious or deceptive in any sense. And I hope this hasn't come across as judgmental or unfeeling. I promise that is not my heart behind this. As a Christian, it is at the core of my belief that all people are bound for hell without Jesus

Christ's gift of salvation. And I don't want you to suffer in hell for all eternity. I would like to see you in heaven someday.

Sincerely,

Nicholas M. Krohn.

ABOUT THE AUTHOR

Nicholas M. Krohn has always had a love for both writing and the Lord. Nicholas received Jesus Christ as his Lord and Saviour at the age of nine, thanks to his faith-filled mother and a godly church. After his salvation, Nicholas spent most of his childhood free-time jotting down fantastical stories that had a deep sense of Christianity within them. When he was a teenager, Nicholas discovered that writing was his calling from God. When attending Heartland Baptist Bible College, Nicholas began seriously writing and self-publishing novels with the desire that they would both wholesomely entertain readers, yet bring glory to God's name. It was here that he met his wife, Marissa, whom he married in 2017. Halfway through college, Nicholas also realized that he could do more than just write Christian Fiction. After deep study in the Bible and graduating from Heartland Baptist Bible College in 2020, Nicholas made it his mission to not only point to the Lord with his fiction novels, but to expound on the Word of God itself through commentaries, in-depth studies, and other such works of literature. Nicholas continues to pursue this work while living in

Iowa with his wife and children.

OTHER WORKS OF THE KROHN FAMILY

(All of which are available on Amazon)

MARISSA KROHN

The Silent Princess (*Children's book*)

NICHOLAS M. KROHN

BIBLE COMMENTARY SERIES

Krohn's Commentary of the Book of Ruth

Krohn's Commentary of the First Book of Samuel

Krohn's Commentary of the Second Book of Samuel

THE SCOEFIELD SERIES (*HISTORICAL FICTION*)

Scoefield

Engel

Blume

THE ZALIAN CHRONICLES (*CHRISTIAN FANTASY*)

Heroes & Thieves I: The Noble Bandit

Heroes & Thieves II: A Bundle of Fools

Heroes & Thieves III: Clapia's Rebirth

Heroes & Thieves IV: Two Wastelands

KROHN'STORIES POETRY

Trains, Bridges, Cups, & Cheese

The Rambling of a Cart Pusher

CONTACT US

Website: krohnstories.storiad.com

Facebook Group: Krohn'Stories Books

Instagram: krohnstoriesbooks

Email: krohnstories@gmail.com

Fan mail, inquiries, suggestions, and critiques are all welcome.

We will do our best to reply to all messages/emails, but cannot

promise due to a busy schedule. Please be appropriate. Any

swearing, vulgarity, threatening, or otherwise inappropriate

messages/emails will be deleted without any response.

www.ingramcontent.com/pod-product-compliance
Lightning Source LLC
Chambersburg PA
CBHW021652120626
46545CB00002B/828